What Are The Elements?

The elements are principle components of all life in the Universe. Everything in creation has a spacial characteristic (Air), a flow characteristic (Water), an electrical characteristic (Fire), and a material characteristic (Earth). These characteristics combined are the forces that compel and propel the infinite existence of Life to keep expanding and expressing itself.

From a metaphysical perspective, these elements symbolize fundamental components of our human existence that influence who and how we are.

The Air Element symbolizes our Mental Awareness.
The Water Element symbolizes our Emotional Awareness.
The Fire Element symbolizes our Creative Awareness.
The Earth Element symbolizes our Physical Awareness.

Why Do We Need This Awareness?

Being aware of how the fundamental components of life affect us helps us to better understand our perceptions, emotions, motivations, and actions. Life operates in balance, and the canvas of nature is a perfect place to observe this balancing act. We can look at nature and the world around us to gain examples of how these elements behave in balance and imbalance. When our elements are imbalanced, our lives become chaotic and unproductive, and we work against the flow of life that leads us to success and prosperity. Building up awareness of Air, Water, Fire, and Earth and their energetic influences in our lives helps us to balance our energies, center ourselves, and live life from a space of cultivated power and wisdom.

How Do We Use This Book?

This guidebook is aligned with the correspondences of the elements and the days of the week. Each day has its own energy and attributes that govern its flow and efficiency. The more you incorporate these energies into your day by taking time to acknowledge and participate in them, the more you will see your days impart productivity and flow in your life.

For each day, I outline elemental symbolism and energies of the day that will help you honor the power of the corresponding element in your life. I also include my own personal practices and suggestions on what you can do to increase awareness of your elements and create balance in your life. Refer to this guidebook often for information on the powers of Air, Water, Fire, and Earth, suggestions and tips on how to honor these energies daily, and wisdom about living in alignment and balance when you honor the elements of your life.

HONOR YOUR AIR ELEMENT ON MONDAY

AIR SYMBOLISM: Intellect, Communication, Intuition

DAY ENERGIES: Inner-reflection, Contemplation, Feminine mysteries

ELEMENTAL COLOR: Yellow

Monday's energy is good for inner-reflection and contemplation. Take some time today to connect to your Intuition. It is a guide and protector, but we often rationalize the voice into barely a whisper.

Are you listening to your thoughts and ponderings that have no visible proof?

Are you following the connecting of dots that network beyond your immediate comprehension?

Like Air, Intuition is an invisible network that allows information to travel between persons, places, and things.

Honor your Air Element by listening to your Intuition.

MY PERSONAL PRACTICE: On Mondays, I honor my Air Element by doing freewriting journaling. I ask myself a question about a personal concern I need insight into, then, I start writing my thoughts without editing them. I write whatever comes to mind until I cannot think of anything else to write. I don't analyze the thoughts while writing. This technique allows me to externalize my thoughts without analysis so I can tap into more subconscious awareness and gain clarity.

HONOR YOUR AIR ELEMENT ON TUESDAY

AIR SYMBOLISM: Perception and Perspective

DAY ENERGIES: Dominance, Courage, Aggression

Are you the authority of your perception & perspective?

Do you consciously decide the viewpoint you take and how you process sensory data?

Honor your Air Element today by evaluating your stance on any subject, but especially one you are opposed to.

Do you see it this way because you consciously concluded so under your own influence, or are you following a conditioned response or programmed train of thought?

You have to dominate your mind's way of thinking through voluntary personal analysis and crafting your own conditioning.

MY PERSONAL PRACTICE: Tuesdays are my day to go to war with myself, so I honor my Air Element by consciously challenging my perspectives. I try to listen to opposing viewpoints, and then step into that perspective to see things from that side. I even ask myself my I think of something the way I do, and trace that line of thinking as far back as I can. This brings awareness to my personal opinions and preferences, and helps me become more self-determined.

To challenge my perception, I like to watch mystery movies and solve riddles. Data can be analyzed in many ways, so it's beneficial to continuously introduce your mind to various ways to perceive data, situations, and circumstances. This expands your options and knowledge so you can be more acutely perceptive.

HONOR YOUR AIR ELEMENT ON WEDNESDAY

AIR SYMBOLISM: Intelligence, Knowledge, Communication

DAY ENERGIES: Education, Study, Writing

Wednesday holds the energy of higher consciousness through educating oneself. It's also highly aligned with the Air Element.

Honor your Air Element today by increasing your skills, cultivating your intelligences, and learning something new. Knowledge builds up perception, perspective, and intuition.

The more you know, the more options you can recognize, letting your reality become a more expansive experience.

Increase your skills, cultivate your intelligence, and learn something new.

MY PERSONAL PRACTICE: Wednesdays are my study days. I make time to do whatever cultivates knowledge and introduces new information:

Take a class
Study my favorite subjects
Watch informative videos
Read chapters from a skill-based book

HONOR YOUR AIR ELEMENT ON THURSDAY

AIR SYMBOLISM: Imagination, Thinking, Vision

DAY ENERGIES: Healing, Expansion, Optimism

The imagination is an aspect of our Air that is dimmed down to a whisper as we age. Very rarely do we cultivate a mindset of curiosity and wonder.

We allow our unhealthy egos to fear not knowing the answers to life's questions. How can we know everything in this vast, infinite existence anyway?

But, with the imagination, we can step into unknown worlds to discover and create from their endless inspiration.

Healing your imagination takes a spirit of playful curiosity and humility in the presence of All That Is. Allow your mind to wander into the irrational, unproven, whimsical darkness of creativity with awe and glee.

MY PERSONAL PRACTICE: I heal my Air Element in imagination by watching animation and fantasy movies. I read about the pioneers of creative imagination and innovation, like Disney and da Vinci. Studying space and even going to a planetarium helps stretch my mind beyond the borders of our earthly atmosphere. I also do creative writing about my future, and allow myself to imagine all the amazing things I will do.

HONOR YOUR AIR ELEMENT ON FRIDAY

AIR SYMBOLISM: Illusion, Change

DAY ENERGIES: Beauty, Transformation, Pleasure

Air symbolizes illusion, glamour, and change. Our mind's love the creativity of a good trick of the eye, admiring the skill involved in optical manipulation.

Since today's energy flows well with self-love, beauty, and pleasure, you can honor Air through enjoying beautification and adornment.

Play in your make-up, get a new haircut, wear something you wouldn't normally wear by dressing up or down in style.

Be creative and alter your appearance in honor of beauty and change.

MY PERSONAL PRACTICE: On Fridays, I honor my Air by dressing up in a creative way. I add a bit more color to my outfits, and wear jewelry I might not normally wear. I dress myself up to invite the energy of beauty into my day.

I also schedule my beauty appointments on Fridays to flow in the energy of change and beautification.

HONOR YOUR AIR ELEMENT ON SATURDAY

AIR SYMBOLISM: Truth, Wisdom, Strategy

DAY ENERGIES: Protection, Revealing Truth, Overcoming Obstacles

Saturday's energy of protection can be expressed through creating strategies on how to handle what you are accountable for, value, invest in, and cherish.

This includes strategizing the way you respond to and maneuver through your life.

You cannot effectively strategize a successful plan if you don't know the truth of the matter. A strategy built on lies and misinformation will crumble and falter.

Tell yourself the truth about where you are in life or what you are dealing with. That is the only way to honor your Air Element with a strong and effective strategy that will produce high results.

MY PERSONAL PRACTICE: Saturdays are my days to power through and get things done. When I start strategizing for any upcoming goal, I first take an honest look and contemplate what I am really dealing with. If it's procrastination, immaturity, pain, jealousy, etc., I find that root and own it. From there, I can develop a plan that is effective based on the truth of what's going on.

HONOR YOUR AIR ELEMENT ON SUNDAY

AIR SYMBOLISM: Breath of Life, Thinking

DAY ENERGIES: Spiritual Connections, Rituals

Sunday's energy is bright, fun, and full of happiness. It works well for taking time to connect with nature and Spirit.

Take time to meditate and connect inward. Focus on your breath, on a sound, or on a word. Acknowledge life in every breath you take.

Allow your mind to travel in and through the meaning and experience of whatever you decide to focus on.

Create a moment of spiritual peace by honoring your Air in meditation and breath.

MY PERSONAL PRACTICE: I like to go into nature on Sundays, so to honor my Air Element I meditate outdoors.

I sit on the ground out in the sun or near a tree, close my eyes, and focus on my breath or on the sounds of birds chirping around me. I let all of my tension flow down into the ground, and connect to the peace in the moment.

AIR ELEMENT WISDOM

Be radically, unapologetically, raw and viciously honest with yourself so you can shatter the illusions of life as you know it.

You are a liar.

You lie to yourself everyday -

About your relationship being what you need... About why your business isn't thriving... About being content with the fantasy of the life you want... About living in 2nd place for family...marriage...job security... About why you don't go hard for yourself, require your worth, command what you want... You are lying to yourself to keep your fears feeding while you zombie walk through life.

If you are going to master the skills of manifestation AND sustainability, you are going to have to tell yourself the truth about how -

You settled for less...
You aren't equipped to love yourself fully and healthily...
You don't like yourself and you don't want to be here anymore...
You like the pain and anguish of struggle because it gets you high...
You want to be saved...
You cannot build on an illusion. That's why things aren't stable and progressing like you want.

Be viciously honest with yourself, and clarity and self-awareness will help you finally get some stuff done.

Get out of your own way.

WATER

HONOR YOUR WATER ELEMENT ON MONDAY

WATER SYMBOLISM: Healing, Cleansing, Purification

DAY ENERGIES: Emotional Healing, Dream Work, Wisdom

ELEMENTAL COLOR: Blue

Monday's energy is highly aligned with the Water Element, and is in flow with investing in our emotional well-being.

Take time to visit your emotions. Trigger an emotional thought or memory and do some freewriting journaling.

Dreams are also a way we process our emotions. Investing in a dream journal helps us connect with our subconscious, intuition, and psychic abilities.

Allow your emotions to talk to and through you so you can gain their wisdom and healing powers.

MY PERSONAL PRACTICE: Mondays are my most emotional days. I allow myself to be triggered by whatever is painful or upsetting, and then I spend time being in that emotional state so I can find clarity and peace.

I cry and allow myself to feel whatever comes up. I don't judge the emotion or suppress it. I embody the emotional energy, and then I journal my thoughts. I focus on feeling, accepting, and releasing emotional energies.

HONOR YOUR WATER ELEMENT ON TUESDAY

WATER SYMBOLISM: Receptive, Flowing, Power

DAY ENERGIES: Sex, Conquest, Male Virility

Tuesday is a day of conquering with power, strength, and high energy. You can heighten connection to your Water Element today by being receptive to sexual and sensual pleasures.

Water has no sharp corners. It receives the shape of whatever contains it, yet is powerful enough to wear down a valley in solid rock. Pleasure is not given; the energy is received, and allowed to flow through channels and filters that interpret it as bliss.

Receive and flow with your sexual pleasures today, so you can experience the sheer power of this life-giving energy.

MY PERSONAL PRACTICE: Tuesdays are great for high energy pleasure; no matter what form I indulge in, I emotionally connect with the moment. Using potent sexual energy to conquer fears or blocks to certain forms of pleasure helps facilitate emotional release.

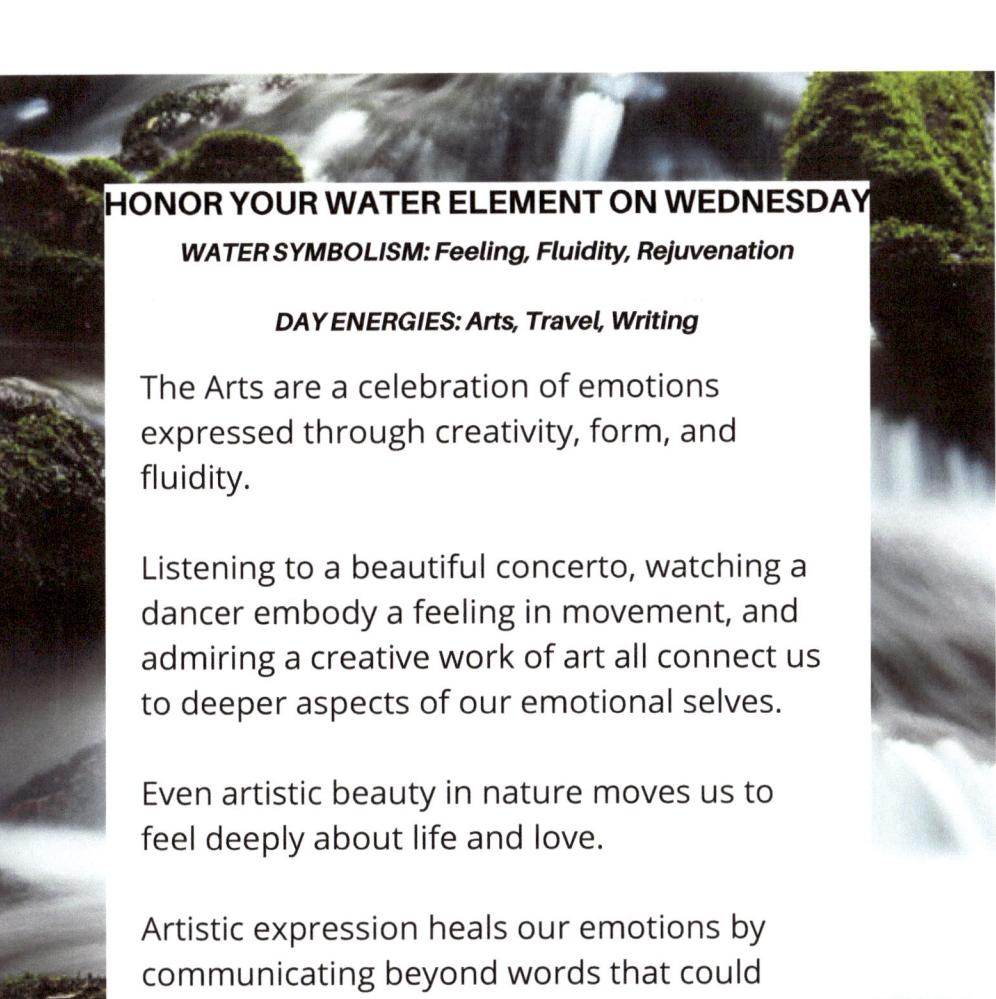

HONOR YOUR WATER ELEMENT ON WEDNESDAY

WATER SYMBOLISM: Feeling, Fluidity, Rejuvenation

DAY ENERGIES: Arts, Travel, Writing

The Arts are a celebration of emotions expressed through creativity, form, and fluidity.

Listening to a beautiful concerto, watching a dancer embody a feeling in movement, and admiring a creative work of art all connect us to deeper aspects of our emotional selves.

Even artistic beauty in nature moves us to feel deeply about life and love.

Artistic expression heals our emotions by communicating beyond words that could describe our highest highs and lowest lows.

Be inspired by what you experience, and let it move you deeply in your heart.

MY PERSONAL PRACTICE: On Wednesdays, I like to travel to a beautiful spot in nature, or go to a museum or theatre. I emotionally connect to the artistic expression by feeling what the artist is expressing. I open up to the beauty of nature, be it a babbling stream or field of flowers, and journal what wants to be expressed through me.

HONOR YOUR WATER ELEMENT ON THURSDAY

WATER SYMBOLISM: Subconscious, Depth, Regeneration

DAY ENERGIES: Abundance, Wealth, Energetic Increase

Energy is stored in thought and memory. Once this energy is released through acceptance and acknowledgement, it is an available increase we can use at will. When you think about being abundant, wealthy, prosperous, optimistic, how do you feel?

Does your mood increase in vibration or decrease? Can you discern the script playing in your mind that is influencing your emotions? What is hidden in the depths of our subconscious greatly impacts our ability to maintain prosperous cycles in life.

We have to invoke emotional awareness by experiencing the feelings words trigger, so we can understand our emotional responses and their roots.

Becoming aware of your emotional responses is a critical step in using the energetic power of your emotions to manifest your desired reality.

MY PERSONAL PRACTICE: When honoring my Water Element on Thursdays, I follow the path of triggering words, thoughts, images, etc. I allow my emotions to come up regarding anything triggering, and I sit with those emotions and follow the path to its origin. Often triggers are not about the catalyst, but rather a deeply anchored emotional thought. Discovering that origin helps regain control of emotional energy.

HONOR YOUR WATER ELEMENT ON FRIDAY

WATER SYMBOLISM: Cleansing, Healing, Calming

DAY ENERGIES: Love, Resolving Relationship Issues, Reconciliation

Friday's energy is ripe with love, happiness, excitement, and fun.

Take some time today to go beyond "date night" expectations, and connect with your partner on an emotionally intimate level.

In a state of calm, make eye contact, hold hands, and talk about what you are experiencing emotionally within your relationship.

Have a therapist, coach, counselor, or spiritual advisor facilitate and even mediate this session for you, so you can both express more in emotion while receiving guidance and wisdom.

Invest time to cleanse the energy in your relationship to help process any unspoken emotions in a healing way that promotes love, growth, and intimacy

MY PERSONAL PRACTICE: The most openly flowing conversations I've had with loved ones has been when we are in a state of relaxation. For my son, it's while we're driving. For my husband, it's when we're in bed right before going to sleep or right after waking up. Emotional maintenance in relationships can be approached from a place of connecting, bonding, and sharing for the edification of the relationship and those involved.

HONOR YOUR WATER ELEMENT ON SATURDAY

WATER SYMBOLISM: Force, Emotional Power

DAY ENERGIES: Self-discipline, Overcoming Obstacles

Self-discipline is as much a matter of emotion (Water) as it is thought (Air) and action (Fire). Emotional energy is a force that can drive you towards or away from the success of your goals. It can power you through the toughest tests of will, or hold you back behind the glass of self-deprecation.

To master self-discipline, you must master how you feel about what must be done, what you are sacrificing to do it, and how you feel about yourself in that process. As you work through the process of becoming disciplined, use your emotional energy, no matter the degree of expression, as a force that helps you push through and accomplish your goals. Water can be used with so much force that it erodes solid material to nothing.

The force of your emotional energies, whether positive or negative, can help shape your life in productive ways if used wisely and purposefully

MY PERSONAL PRACTICE: Disciplining myself led to an ability to harness my emotional energy and use it for a beneficial purpose. When I am upset, I do something that will benefit me like go for a walk, organize or clean up, or write in my journal. I don't turn that energy on myself in a detrimental way that I'll have to recover from or fix later on. I value myself and my progress more than emotional gratification, so I use my energy to my advantage.

HONOR YOUR WATER ELEMENT ON SUNDAY

WATER SYMBOLISM: Devotion, Rebirth, Hydration

DAY ENERGIES: Health Consciousness, Nature, Wealth

Nature is our first healer. She is the master of destruction and rebirth, plentiful in healing remedies, and keeping us alive with Her wealth of replenished resources.

Take time to commune with Nature near water. Engulf yourself in the blue waves of the ocean. Hike a forest lake trail. Enjoy the sun on a sandy beach.

Nature is refreshing to our spirit. Allow the glassy reflection of its mirror to show you more of who you are as you recharge and rehydrate in natural beauty and splendor.

MY PERSONAL PRACTICE: I love going to the beach to commune with nature and rejuvenate. I walk out into the waves and release all my tensions and concerns. Water adds a feeling of abundance to my sense of well-being, so I take pleasure in being around lakes and streams while walking and hiking in parks and forests.

WATER ELEMENT WISDOM

Emotional words are powerful, and used authentically, create opportunities to be supported. When you cry out from the storm of your emotions, allow yourself to be witnessed, heard, and fortified in that moment.

I've experienced personal moments where I've spoken through sobbing tears to express my pain.

In those moments, space was created for me to be witnessed, acknowledged, and supported. It was created because I showed up bravely and authentically in vulnerability.

But, even in being witnessed, often the others did not have the capacity to support me.

And, in some of those moments, I was alone, supporting the fragmented persona within myself. So, I basically talked through myself to myself from two different aspects.

The most important part was that I showed up in that moment for me.

I learned to fortify myself with love and acceptance, and honor my emotions with authentic expression without expectation, and regardless of someone else's response.

FIRE

HONOR YOUR FIRE ELEMENT ON MONDAY

FIRE SYMBOLISM: Action, Movement, Activity

DAY ENERGIES: Home & Family Life, Inner Healing Rituals

ELEMENTAL COLOR: Red

Fire Element honor on Mondays is well-served by tending to inner dwelling upkeep, both structurally and bodily.

We probably look begrudgingly at returning to work on Mondays because the energy of the day is very feminine (inwardly focused) and best utilized working on self/home cleansing and organization.

Today is a good day to handle home errands and chores, as well as deal with any family issues or activities.

Honor your Fire by doing inner Self work, especially any emotional cleansing rituals to heal trauma and recalibrate emotional gauges.

MY PERSONAL PRACTICE: Mondays are my day to do home errands and work on inner self maintenance. Whatever errands or chores need to be done for my household, I do them on Mondays. I also take time to do any rituals or practices that help me heal my inner self, like burning incense and candles, and playing peaceful meditative music all day. I use the energy of Mondays to boost what I do to keep my home and inner self flowing productively.

HONOR YOUR FIRE ELEMENT ON TUESDAY

FIRE SYMBOLISM: Will, Courage

DAY ENERGIES: Aggression, Initiation, Victory

Your will is comprised of desire, self-determination, and self-actualization.

When you courageously pursue your goals and wants, despite fear or apprehension, you stoke your inner flame.

A fire-fueled life is initiated through doing what you want to do, how you want to do it, when you want to do it.

Use today to do something you've always wanted to do. Face your fears and make it happen.

The feeling of victorious accomplishment sets your life-fire ablaze to experience more.

MY PERSONAL PRACTICE: Tuesdays are my days to challenge my fears and apprehensions and move courageously towards what I want. After observing an emotional, inwardly focused Monday, I focus Tuesday's energy on fueling my agenda with all of my freed up energy. The feeling of accomplishing a task or goal that may have been blocked by fear or insecurity just hypes me up to do more of what I want to do the way I want to do it.

HONOR YOUR FIRE ELEMENT ON WEDNESDAY

FIRE SYMBOLISM: Illumination, Ambition, Creativity

DAY ENERGIES: Study, Answers, Education

Goals and aspirations can feel like lofty undertakings when you get started.

You have to become informed about your goal and what you have to do to achieve it.

Strategizing a plan to achieve a goal requires knowledge of processes and options. You must know what to do in the field of your goal so your actions lead to success.

Use today's energy of study and education to gain knowledge and be informed about your goal. Seek information to answer questions you may have, and prepare for developing a plan of action.

MY PERSONAL PRACTICE: What I do to honor fire on Wednesdays is study, study, study. I research and study as much information as I can on my goals and what the process to achieve them involves. I might have to gain a new skill, do some networking, get a mentor, etc. Educating myself on the arena of my goal helps me devise a plan that will propel my actions in a successful direction.

HONOR YOUR FIRE ELEMENT ON THURSDAY

FIRE SYMBOLISM: Energy, Freedom, Motivation

DAY ENERGIES: Increase, Prosperity, Expansion

Volcano lava erupts from fiery depths with molten drive to create and expand the territory and reach of the mountain. In order for your Life-Flame to burn high and bright, it must be fueled.

Today, feed your motivation to experience more freedom in your life. Expand yourself by traveling, doing something new or challenging, and investing energy in what makes you feel free in life.

Let fiery motivation drive you to expand yourself and create the freedom you desire in life.

MY PERSONAL PRACTICE: I honor Fire on Thursdays by doing and experiencing new things. It might be as elaborate as going to an event or as simple as finding a new route home. As long as I am breaking out of routine and expanding my awareness of the infinite options available to me, I am fueling a sense of freedom and motivation to live life more fully.

HONOR YOUR FIRE ELEMENT ON FRIDAY

FIRE SYMBOLISM: Passion, Arousal

DAY ENERGIES: Pleasure, Love, Social Activities

Passion is a high voltage energy that must be cultivated.

Your passions are creative outlets that produce excitement, curiosity, joy, and arouse lust for living and enjoying life's pleasures.

Today, get together with friends and partake in activities that fuel your passion and creative impulses.

Investing energy in doing things that cultivate the enticement of your senses feeds passion and stirs arousal to produce pleasurably and positively in your life.

MY PERSONAL PRACTICE: TGIF!!! Mixing fellowship with creative activities is an awesome way to bond and create memorable experiences. A group outing to a cooking class or a fun Paint-N-Wine class sparks our passion to create with pleasure. Karaoke night stirs up passion to perform and entertain, so have some creative fun!

HONOR YOUR FIRE ELEMENT ON SATURDAY

FIRE SYMBOLISM: Purification, Destruction

DAY ENERGIES: Tough Love, Ending What No Longer Works

The self-discipline energy of Saturday is perfect for some tough love shadow work.

It's always better to get on your own ass and work on getting out of your own way before the Universal energies do it for you.

Fire destroys what no longer holds energy to feed it. You are the Eternal Flame of Life. Let yourself by purified and galvanized into a stronger, higher expression of Self.

Put yourself in the Ring of Fire and allow the flame of truth to purify and burn up what's been holding you back.

MY PERSONAL PRACTICE: On Saturdays I increase my self-discipline by working on my limiting habits and beliefs, building consistency in my productive habits, and taking care of the tasks that may not be that much fun, but contribute to accomplishing my goals. I sacrifice fun and relaxation on Saturday to build successful habits and progress.

HONOR YOUR FIRE ELEMENT ON SUNDAY

FIRE SYMBOLISM: Sun Energy, Transformation, Life Force

DAY ENERGIES: Power, Personal Achievement, Success

Sunday's bright and cheerful energy is great for celebrating and appreciating Life. You may know and understand you have power to transform your life, but how often do you celebrate that?

Do you take time to celebrate your success of transforming yourself and your reality? Have you acknowledged your achievements, and honored yourself in all the hard work and dedication you've invested?

Completing a fiery life initiation, and rising from the ashes of an old you like a mythical Phoenix, is cause to celebrate your personal power to change your life for the better.

MY PERSONAL PRACTICE: I had to learn to appreciate my successes without resting in them. I take time to celebrate and acknowledge my life transformations and accomplishments, and appreciate all the hard work I have done, so I can stay motivated to keep progressing and elevating my life according to my vision.

FIRE ELEMENT WISDOM

A well-pruned life holds the brightest fire.

Fire is an energy not easily contained or influenced. It consumes everything in its path. In studying fire, I've learned about how it lives and breathes through feeding. When fire is feeding, it can consume so thoroughly that it begins to die if there is no substance left to give it energy.

Take a candle wick, for example. A candle flame can become smothered in liquid wax if the wick is not tended to consistently. It will melt wax faster than it can consume the wax as fuel. The flame will burn low and eventually be overwhelmed. But, once you trim that wick, and remove the dead, consumed material that no longer feeds the bridge between flame and fuel, the flame instantly brightens and burns high and strong.

Life may feel like it's knocking you around, cutting off familiar connections and situations, but it's really trimming away the dead, consumed parts that no longer feed your life force. If your life is burning low with lost passion, lethargy, lack of creativity, start cutting off what's weighing you down and no longer feeding your lust for life.

Then, feed your life flame with new goals, new pleasures, new adventures.

EARTH

HONOR YOUR EARTH ELEMENT ON MONDAY

EARTH SYMBOLISM: Grounding, Fertility, Nurturing

DAY ENERGIES: Rituals, Feminine Health

ELEMENTAL COLOR: Green

Earth Element energy is nurturing and grounding, which connects us to our center.

For women, our womb holds our feminine power and essence. We have to care for our wombs and nurture the flow of energy through us that feeds our sensuality, sexuality,and creativity.

Take some time today to enjoy the world around you as you tend to your inner self-care, so you can center, recalibrate, and realign with Self.

Everyone can benefit from connecting with the Earth to nurture a more present awareness in ourselves and the world around us.

MY PERSONAL PRACTICE: Today is excellent for feminine womb care, like yoni steaming, womb meditation, or yoni rituals for self-awareness and healthy upkeep. I take time to connect skin to skin with Nature by walking barefoot in the grass, leaning against or hugging a tree, or just standing in the sun for a few minutes.

HONOR YOUR EARTH ELEMENT ON TUESDAY

EARTH SYMBOLISM: Order, Bounty, Resources

DAY ENERGIES: Protection, Strength

The Earth is bountiful with gemstones, crystals, precious metals, and other valuable substances. These treasures are typically hidden below ground and in cave dwellings, protected from easy access.

We too house hidden treasures of gifts, talents, and ideas that are resources we can use to progress and profit our lives. Just as it takes great effort and energy to unearth and collect valuable resources, so does it take effort and energy to cultivate your skills and talents and enrich your life with them.

Take time today to set yourself in order about your gifts and talents. Are you using them? Why not, or how can you strengthen them if you are? What natural resources do you possess that could be increasing your life and adding value to others? Why are you wasting your resources on those who don't appreciate them? (Appreciate also means to INCREASE in value)

You are valuable. Your body is a valuable vessel housing hidden treasures and talents. Personal strategy is a protection plan for what you value when you know your worth, and keeps you focused on productivity with your cultivated resources.

Recognize your value, and strategize to use your gifts and talents productively. Don't give yourself away, and waste your resources on the undeserving

HONOR YOUR EARTH ELEMENT ON WEDNESDAY

EARTH SYMBOLISM: Prosperity, Stability

DAY ENERGIES: Knowledge, Study, Self-Improvement

Earth that is tended to gainfully produces.

Your body and your finances represent physical manifestations of earthly materials. The more you know about how both of these vehicles work, the more efficiently and successfully you can use them.

Take time today to study and increase your knowledge and understanding of building stable results in your fitness and financial goals. This will help your plan of action be more profitable, and your results more sustainable.

Longevity in your fitness and finances results requires knowledge of how to be profitable with your invested energy.

MY PERSONAL PRACTICE: To strengthen my Earth Element in fitness and finance, I study how to improve and increase my dexterity and abilities in both areas. I've talked with fitness trainers, practiced various fitness regimens, and increased my knowledge of nutrition that works for me.

I also educate myself on financial planning and management so I can control, grow, and manage my money and resources to increase them productively.

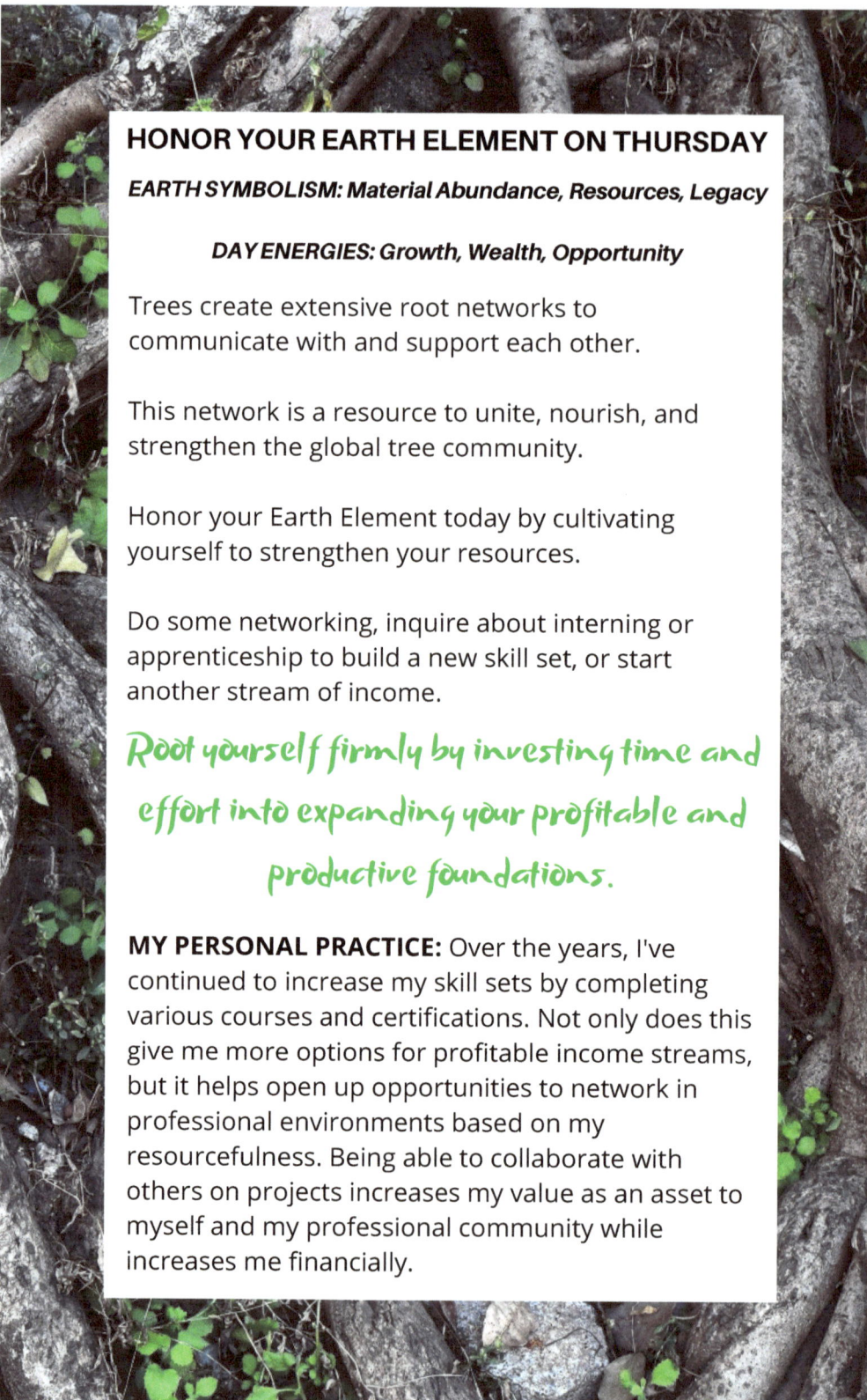

HONOR YOUR EARTH ELEMENT ON THURSDAY

EARTH SYMBOLISM: Material Abundance, Resources, Legacy

DAY ENERGIES: Growth, Wealth, Opportunity

Trees create extensive root networks to communicate with and support each other.

This network is a resource to unite, nourish, and strengthen the global tree community.

Honor your Earth Element today by cultivating yourself to strengthen your resources.

Do some networking, inquire about interning or apprenticeship to build a new skill set, or start another stream of income.

Root yourself firmly by investing time and effort into expanding your profitable and productive foundations.

MY PERSONAL PRACTICE: Over the years, I've continued to increase my skill sets by completing various courses and certifications. Not only does this give me more options for profitable income streams, but it helps open up opportunities to network in professional environments based on my resourcefulness. Being able to collaborate with others on projects increases my value as an asset to myself and my professional community while increases me financially.

HONOR YOUR EARTH ELEMENT ON FRIDAY

EARTH SYMBOLISM: Nature, Nourishment, Recycling

DAY ENERGIES: Beauty, Pleasure, Fertility

Everything we experience is sourced and materialized from the lush beauty and ample nourishment of the Earth. Our bodies are enlivened by all of the tastes, smells, sounds, sights, and feels in this sensory wonderland.

Celebrate today by enjoying sensual pleasures of delicious foods, beautiful greenery, aromatic flowers, and all of the amazing creations on Earth's canvas.

Energize your body with the delightfully sensual array of beauty this abundant planet has to offer.

MY PERSONAL PRACTICE: The beauty of nature is a potent way to energize your body. I energize my senses by wearing my favorite perfume, or eating my favorite cuisine. I feed myself with all of my senses by experiencing the beauty of art, food, aromas, and sensations. My life is robust and nourishing because I indulge in the abundant beauty of Earth.

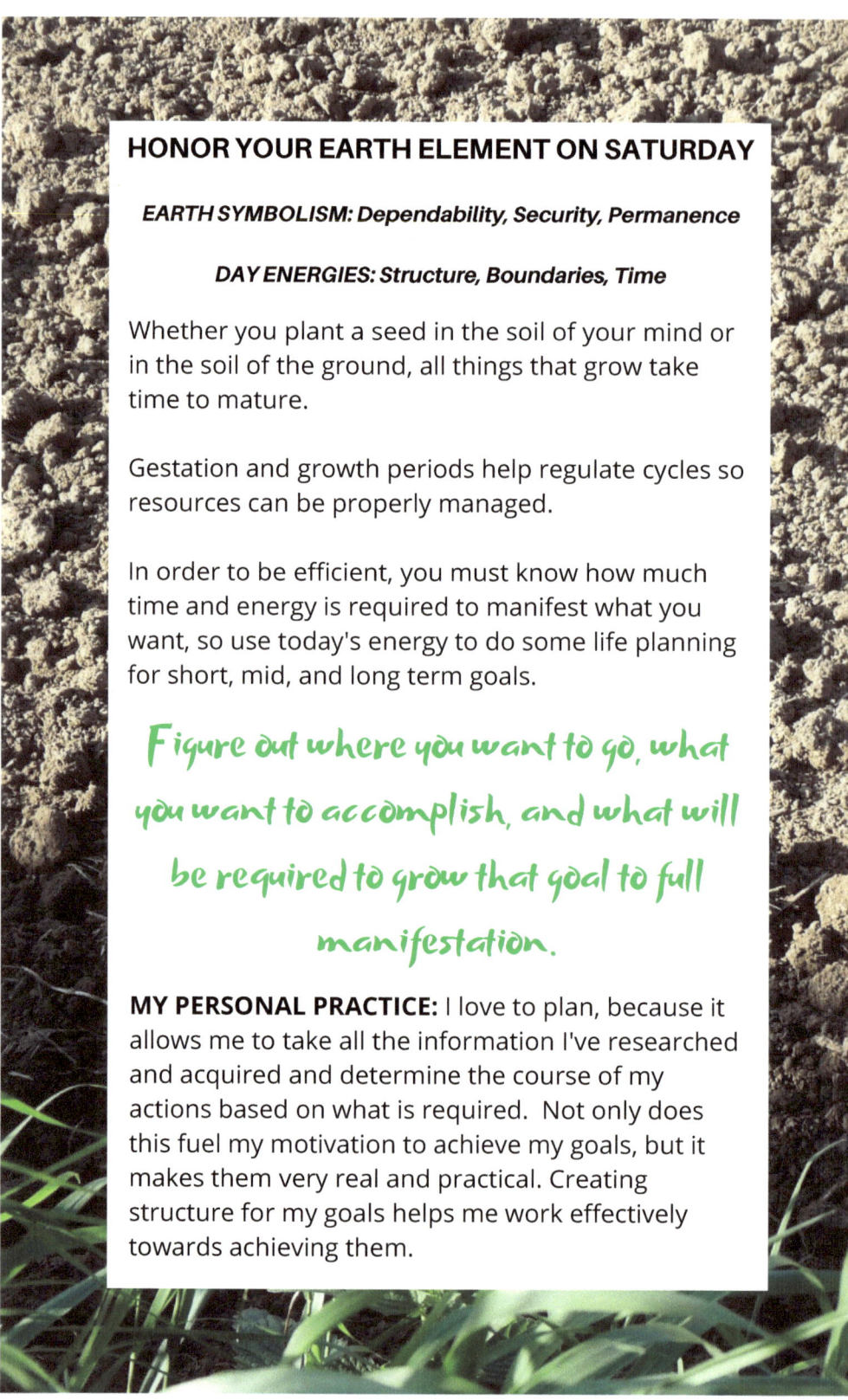

HONOR YOUR EARTH ELEMENT ON SATURDAY

EARTH SYMBOLISM: Dependability, Security, Permanence

DAY ENERGIES: Structure, Boundaries, Time

Whether you plant a seed in the soil of your mind or in the soil of the ground, all things that grow take time to mature.

Gestation and growth periods help regulate cycles so resources can be properly managed.

In order to be efficient, you must know how much time and energy is required to manifest what you want, so use today's energy to do some life planning for short, mid, and long term goals.

Figure out where you want to go, what you want to accomplish, and what will be required to grow that goal to full manifestation.

MY PERSONAL PRACTICE: I love to plan, because it allows me to take all the information I've researched and acquired and determine the course of my actions based on what is required. Not only does this fuel my motivation to achieve my goals, but it makes them very real and practical. Creating structure for my goals helps me work effectively towards achieving them.

HONOR YOUR EARTH ELEMENT ON SUNDAY

EARTH SYMBOLISM: Nature, Creativity, Variety

DAY ENERGIES: Active Living, Success

Nature is full of variety. It's creative force loves to mix itself together and produce something new.

Within those new creations are unlimited expressions of beauty, purpose, and pleasure.

The bright and sunny energy of Sunday is full of fun and movement. It's perfect for going out and exploring the variety of Earth.

Today, enjoy some time in a local park or nature reserve. Visit a beautiful garden. Eat some cuisine you've never had before. Take a walk in nature.

Enjoy the pleasures, nourishment, and creative variety the Earth has to offer, and recharge your Earth Element as a creative, fertile, sensual, productive being.

EARTH ELEMENT WISDOM

You are the strongest, most stable and dependable foundation you can build on.

You are the strongest, most stable, most dependable, most integral substance from which you can build your life.

Just as no material is sourced for our use outside of the Earth and known Universe, nothing is sourced in your life outside of you.

When we try to build on what is fleeting, like jobs, businesses, relationships, successes, skills, and the like, we affix permanence to that which is temporary - just look at the amount of great and powerful civilizations that are as rubble and memory in the belly of the seas.

YOU are what secures you.
Not your money.
Not your employment position.
Not your business.
Not your relationships.

It's your knowledge, wisdom, understanding, thoughts, beliefs, and strategies, all culminating in who you are, that makes for your solid foundation.

Invest your time and energy in cultivating, empowering, and expanding the most secure foundation in your universe - YOURSELF.

www.ingramcontent.com/pod-product-compliance
Lightning Source LLC
Chambersburg PA
CBHW050907290526
45792CB00002B/729